I Love You-Dad Forever!!!!

**A Dad's Love, words or wisdom & Papa bear protection over his children and family far exceeds powerful.
It is Eternal.**

Ann Marie Kim

Balboa Press books may be ordered through booksellers or by contacting:

Balboa Press
A Division of Hay House
1663 Liberty Drive
Bloomington, IN 47403
www.balboapress.com
844-682-1282

ISBN: 979-8-7652-4685-6 (sc)
ISBN: 979-8-7652-4686-3 (hc)
ISBN: 979-8-7652-4684-9 (e)

Library of Congress Control Number: 2023920845

Print information available on the last page.

Balboa Press rev. date: 12/11/2023

BALBOA.PRESS
A DIVISION OF HAY HOUSE

INTRODUCTION

This book is dedicated to the precious memory of my father, James Earl Smith born on May 10, 1942 in Kelford, North Carolina and passed away the evening of March 18, 2022 in Boston, Massachusetts.

Dad, no one prepares you for three (3) things in life; (1) How to stay married after the wedding; (2) How to grieve the loss of your love one and (3) How to sit by and support your Dad, as he has decided not to be resuscitated if he is no longer able to breathe.

My wish for those precious souls reading this book, is that if you have not had the honor already, let your parents know just how much you love them. Thank your Dad for being the best Dad he knew how to be. Spend time doing what your Dad likes to do, for me, my Dad loved to go fishing. Walden Pond was one of his favorite spots along with going Deep Sea Fishing off of Cape Cod Massachusetts. These are some of my fondest memories as well as listening to his wise words of wisdom about life.

Take a moment and bask in the beauty of the gift of your parents. I believe God gives us our parents on loan to show us how to live our lives here on earth. Then, at the appointed time, calls our love ones home to heaven. Thank you Dad for being such a great listener, teacher and genius. You literally could fix anything and always reminded me that I may accomplish anything that I set my mind to.

This Morning 1-28-2023

Good morning, Dad! You may have no idea how much we all miss you and Mom! During my quiet-time with God this morning, reading the Bible, sitting quietly to allow the Holy Spirit to speak to my soul….I wrote this down in my journal and thought, I need to include these words in this book, God has placed on my heart to honor you. Thank You, God for blessing my life with such great parents. Both my Mom & Dad's love for me carries me throughout this lifetime. God, what a Gift You have bestowed upon my Soul, oh Lord, My God! My heart overflows with Eternal Gratitude, Forever!!!!!

Cat Food

Dad, I am not sure how Heaven works, or if you are able to read this book from there, or listen to my thoughts as I write this book? Yesterday morning, as I was making my bed, I started to laugh. I thought, oh, how I wish Dad were here so I could call him and share this funny story about the Cat Food with him. Four (4) months after you passed away to be with The Lord, a feral cat showed up on my door step. She was meowing, asking for food. I thought, if I feed her, she will constantly come back and not hunt the mice on the property. So, instead of placing more scraps of food out, I shared with her how important it is for her to learn how to hunt. I explained that there are acres and acres of land out there with tons of mice for her taking. I think she understood, as she walked away. Three (3) days later, she showed back up again. Now, Dad, the first time she appeared, I thought wow, this cat is so skinny. When she came by again, I said to myself, Lord, I must feed her. I would feel guilty if she passed away.

The same day I went and purchased cat food and milk. As I looked out the window, I noticed three (3) little fur balls next to her, all eating from the same bowls of cat food and milk. Everything made sense, the reason why she was not hunting was because she had three (3) little kittens who had to be only a month or so old . Naturally, she had no intention of leaving her kittens unprotected. Living out in the country is amazing. God has and continues to give me the opportunity to have a 'front seat' to nature. These animals are exceedingly wise and intelligent.

Upon watching her and her kittens each day, feed on the food, I praise God for providing for me so that I may be generous to them. (Thank you Dad, I know you were praying for me to have a great job a year or more before you passed away to be with the Lord). I realized, I had something to look forward to, some little pets to care for….as I no longer had you and Mom in the physical form to care for, fuss over and love.

Oh, by the way, Dad, these feral cats are truly Gorgeous! God could not have sent more beautiful cats. The mother, I have named Mulatto, as she is white with black around her ears, eyes and one side of her head. Her daughter, who is a calico cat, I named Mia, after me, as this was the name Johnny would call me when he was a little boy, as he could not pronounce my full name, Ann Marie. Mia is three (3) different colors (white, black and honey colored) which symbolically matches my nationality of three different races. (Italian, African American & Cherokee Indian). The second kitten I named Fluffanetta, as she is so beautiful, with a fluffy white coat, caramel and peanut butter colored tail and similar color around her eyes and ears. Remember, when we were all kids, you used to feed us fluffy white marshmallow spread with peanut butter? She reminds me of a fluffanetta and peanutbutter sandwich.

Yum! Back to the story about the Cat Food. So, since the cats have shown up on my property, there has not been a mouse within the garage within a twenty (20) mile radius. (Laugh out Loud). My best buddy who used to drop by often, has not had to come over to remove mice for some time. He does come over to feed the cats when I travel out of town, however, normally, I do not see him much as the mouse population is now under control thanks to the cats. These cats found an entrance to my chicken coup, where the mice used to 'take up residence' . Now the cats perch in the windows during cold snowy days.

One day, as I finished my dinner and sat down to watch a show, I noticed head lights coming down the driveway and wondered who was coming over for a visit, as I was not expecting company. I turn on the porch light and there is my buddy, standing there with a large bag of cat food. I look at him with a puzzled look on my face and ask why he purchased cat food. He said, 'actually, I found this at the end of my driveway.' I said, what? He explained how someone must have drove by in a truck with the cat food in the rear bed, it slipped off and fell in front of his driveway. He left it there for six (6) hours thinking that perhaps the person would notice that the cat food was missing and go back to trace his/her steps to find it. However, no one ever came back for it.

So, he picked up this heavy bag of cat food and placed it in his garage. He said, he has had it there for three days and finally made time to bring it over. I laughed so hard, Dad. As I believe God has such a sense of humor! God allows a huge bag of cat food to land in front of my best friends place, the one who for all these years has come by my house to remove mice out of the mouse traps, in my garage.

God is showing my friend how He can provide for all things. My friend is going through some health issues and I pray for him and his significant other to believe that God can heal him completely. Dad, on some spiritual level, I believe God is working on my friends heart to say, if I can send you an enormous bag of cat food for your friends feral cats, I can certainly take care of you and heal you completely. Isn't that an amazing story? God always works in powerful ways. I encourage those reading these words to be willing to stop all of the extra chatter in our hearts and souls and breathe in the beauty of miracles unfolding all around us.

This is why I love living here out in the country. There is ample time for quiet reflection and listening to God direct my steps. I have learned over the years, if I do not feel God's peace over a situation, not to move forward. I am leaning in and listening closer now. Like the picture of the Last Supper, where the disciples are leaning in to listen to Jesus. I am on a journey to only lean in and allow God to take my hand down the illuminated Path He has created specifically for me.

What has been amazing to witness is all of the other animals on my property that show up to eat the cat food at night. (Doe, fawns, rabbits, squirrels, opossums and recently, one of the largest raccoons I have ever laid eyes on.) During the day, I noticed even blue jays and ravens swoop down on my deck for a quick meal. Especially, when the feral cats are off climbing trees and playing in the tall grass. Amazing, simply amazing. As winter approached, I have taken in the milk and cat food each night as I have witnessed the opossum eating up all of the food. One is not very friendly to Mia. My neighbor, who has been raised on his family farm right next door, said that opossums are filled with diseases and that I need to get rid of them. Apparently, several of his horses passed away, upon consuming hay that the opossum relieved itself on.

A week or so after you passed away, you appeared in my dream. The dream seemed so real, I thought it actually occurred. It is amazing how the spirit world works. You were in your early twenties, standing in my guest bed room with the riffle we just gave to the police officers as we cleaned out your beautiful place .

I was in awe to see you standing there with the riffle positioned in your hands stating that I am going to need this. Then, I woke up. As I shared the dream with my neighbors daughter and son-in-law, Remember, you had the opportunity to speak with him a couple of times on the phone. He invited you to join him in fishing and ice-fishing adventures. Well, he came over a couple of times with his young boys and shot two (2) of the opossums, as I refused to kill anything. Then, as I thought there were none left on my property, two (2) more appeared.

It has been said that if you do not leave food out, they will move on to another property.   I wish them well and lift up prayers of gratitude for God to move them onto another adventure. I desire for my wild turkeys to come back and nest on the property, as I have discovered that the opossum tends to eat the eggs of these animals. I wish I had asked you more about this animal when you were alive, you would always say someone was 'playing possum' by pretending to be asleep.

Your Pheasant

This past spring was truly special, as like 'clock work' the pheasant showed up on my property, calling to the females and marking his territory. I immediately thought of you as tears welled up in my eyes. Practically, during ever FaceTime call you inquired, "how is my phesant'. He no longer pecks at the sliding door window. I think the feral cats may be the reason why, as Mulatto sun-baths on that deck. I have also asked my neighbor not to hunt him as he was your favorite. I have noticed that the feral cats and the pheasant peacefully co-exist. Each precious animal plays a particular role in nature and I have decided to allow the opossums to remain, as they are most helpful in consuming ticks.

Each day of life is a gift. My finishing this book is bringing about the healing my heart needs. Please forgive me, Dad, for months, I could not sit down and write, as I just did not want to face the fact and pain that you are no longer with us in human form. Now, I have made a vow to God to finish your book by this weekend.

I am one hundred (100%) percent confident, that you would want me (Jimmy, Johnny, Annette, Fervin, Sr and little Fervin, along with the rest of our family and my friends you have met, Dana, Rikki and Tatyana) to live this beautiful life God has given us. This is exactly what I am doing now. Each day is filled with love, happiness, inspiration and purpose. I wish to encourage countless precious souls everywhere on celebrating the lives of those so priceless to them. I pray this book will help them to navigate their way through the grieving process and find peace in knowing that their love one is in a better place. I remember sitting by your bedside and wishing I could take the pain away from your bones. You were in so much pain, barely able to breath, your limbs experiencing atrophy, I praise God you are in a better place now. No more pain, no more tears.

Baking

Dad, I also want you to know (ha ha ha), I have baked homemade biscuits, breads, bagels, and now cookies that are excellent, gluten free and vegan. You remember how you used to tease me years ago about my baking. Well, as your little grand son says often, I did it! Yeah, I did it. I bake exceedingly well now, to match the exceptional cooking abilities that I am confident I inherited from you and Mom! I love you Dad, FOREVER! Thank you for being the best Dad Ever.

Leaving Us

Dad, I knew you were leaving us when you did not want to speak with my friend Rikki on the phone. You treated her like one of your daughters and always had a kind word. I cannot even begin to imagine how challenging it was for you to decide to leave. Unlike Mom, who passed away during the early hours of the morning. You decided to no longer have the breathing apparatus and shared with me how you did not want to die. Torn between the two choices, I stressed how at any time you had the opportunity to decide to have the surgery and live. I even planned to purchase a home on the East Coast to help take good care of you. Instinctively, we both knew that the one surgery would never replace a broken heart. No one could ever take Mom's place. Nothing compared to her and even though everyone grieves differently, we all witnessed this in your eyes, speech and in your heart these last four (4) years, you did not wish to live any longer without her.

Unshakable Faith

I know I mentioned these words to you on countless occasions, however, I wish for the future generations to read and speak these words out loud. God, I believe You can Heal my Dad and allow him to walk again, be strong and vibrant again. God, I want you to know that I have the faith to walk through this journey with my Dad. Because, as the Bible teaches us, over and over again, Jesus healed those who needed to be healed.

Dad, I know you wanted to go, I know you were living with a broken heart over the past four (4) years . Nothing can replace true love. You met when you were sixteen (16) years old. It is as if a part of you passed away with Mom. Dad, you know what I think is beautiful, God sent you Mom, as you did not have a family. You were raised by your uncle, who we all knew as Grandpa. He was a truly wonderful man as well. Yes, everything in life happens for a reason. We may not always understand it as we are moving through the pain, sadness and heart break of loosing you, however, I know you are in a better place, no longer in pain and for this I Praise God.

Fishing

Dad this particular time (although we spent many weekends and days fishing), I came home for a visit with this beautiful purple hat and you said it was so bright and colorful that it would scar away all of the fish. Ha! We both know what happened, I caught calico bass upon calico bass that day and another fellow fisherman came over and said, hum, we know who the true fisherman of the family is. I explained how God ordered the fish to bite the worm on my line, as each was attracted to my beautiful hat.

All of us laughed so hard and I explained to the fisherman how much you kept teasing me about my hat and how the fish were going to swim away. Remember the other time when a snapping turtle caught my fishing line, whew, it was a good thing you knew to cut the line. I'll always treasure our time deep sea fishing off of Cape Cod, I was just learning how to develop my 'sea legs' and after the struggle with catching the baby shark with yourself and several others holding onto me to prevent me from toppling over into the ocean, I went upstairs and fell asleep on the upper deck, away from the choppy waters.

I caught such a sun burn, I felt like a lobster. Dad, there is something about being by the water, whether a pond or the ocean, fishing by your side. Now, what do I do, I do not have anyone to bait my hook. I never liked the worms or small fish that had to be attached for bait. The bible teaches us to be 'fisher's of men'. Dad, I shall always cherish and honor God for saving you. I am so truly grateful for having the honor of God answering my prayer and not allowing you to pass away before I got to see you. God is so faithful, he allowed you to live for five (5) months, until you made the hard, yet very brave decision to no longer have help if you had trouble breathing.

<u>Great Faith</u>

Dad, I know that your heart's desire is for myself and the rest of our family to live the life God has so graciously given us. I was astonished to hear you say to myself and Annette, 'See you on the other side'.

Dad, three years ago, when Mom left us, I believe you decided back then that life, for you, was no longer worth living. Listening to you describe how much you love and miss her was both beautiful and heartbreaking to hear at the same time.

I applaud you Dad, you did the best you could over those years, I cannot even begin to imagine the loss you felt, loosing the love of your life.

Tethered

Dad, you asked me while you were in the hospital at Tufts Medical Center, if you had been a bad person over your lifetime and if this is why this has happened to you. As I said by your bedside and am stating again now, you were not a bad person and I do not know why you had such a bad fall and injured your neck. It pained us to see you laying there not able to talk, or move your arms, hands, legs, feet.

Our gentle giant, no longer here, sometimes, in life, we do not understand why things happen, however, I am convinced of this, God has each one of us in the Palm of His hands and works with our souls to save us. Dad, I am convinced you are smiling in heaven just like you did while here on earth with Mom by your side as she looks on in this picture of you showing us the fish you caught.

Happy Day of Fishing with the love of his life by his side.

Pictures and dreams bring my mind back to a more simpler time. Life, the journey, those precious to your hearts and soul, Dad, I miss you terribly. Sometimes, I wish there was an escalator to heaven, so I may talk with God to fix you and Mom and send you both back to us in perfect health and happiness, like days gone by. On the previous page, there is a picture of a cross tied to a fishing hook you had on the door frame to your bedroom. I love this, as it speaks of your love for God & fishing.

-Journey

Dad, honestly, I really find it quite challenging to write this book. Writing a book about you means that you are no longer here which makes my heart sad. I miss your smile, your stories and asking how your pheasant is doing. (which by the way, he is doing fine). I have asked my neighbors to no longer hunt him as he reminds me so much of our conversations and you constantly asking about him. My neighbors gave me such a beautiful card to honor your life. Matt and his friends really wanted to go fishing and ice-fishing with you and have a couple of beer's.

The Mercy Seat

Two days prior to your passing, I noticed your mouth moving, as though you were having a conversation with someone. I leaned in to catch a glimpse at what you were discussing, however, I could not hear a word. I knew instinctively you were having a conversation with God. You were sitting in the mercy seat, reviewing your life with the King of the Universe.

Initially, I tapped your shoulder to prompt you to wake up. You stopped talking for a moment and opened your eyes…saying, I'll be back, closed your eyes again and starting having this conversation. I am in total Awe and have immense gratitude to God for the process of life, the gift of granting all of us (my siblings) such a Dad.

I prayed to God and asked if this was what was occurring and an ever so gentle thought in my soul said, Yes, He is speaking with God and reviewing his life to prepare his soul to come into heaven. I noticed a similar instance two(2) days before Mom went to be with the Lord, as well. The soul has the honor to sit in the mercy seat, reviewing the time spent down here on earth with the Creator of the Universe. Wow! What a kind and compassionate God we serve, who is so fair and just, allowing us to review our life and how we lived prior to entering heaven.

Dad, I know I am speaking on behalf of all of us you left behind, we miss you beyond words may humanly express.

For so long, we attempted to persuade you to have the minor surgery, however, just like you told the Doctor when you decided not have any more life support, she asked you did you think about this Mr. Smith. You looked at her and said, I have been in this bed for five (5) months, I have had plenty of time to think about it. I loved your meekness, logic and ability to express your thoughts so succinctly with such an audience. There was a room full of doctor's and specialist that day and even though I wanted you to stay with us, I could see your determination in your eyes that you had already decided to take the journey along the streets of gold. I admire your courage and bravery to this day.

Pants & Walking Shoes

Upon completing your conversation with God on the Mercy Seat, prior to your going up to heaven to be with the Lord, you asked me if I had your pants and walking shoes. I can hear your voice, "I do not like them messing with me down there'. Meaning, you prefer that they not clean you, as you were and I am certain most people are used to having their health and not accustomed to having to rely on nurses to clean their lower regions. You asked me if I had your pants, and I said yes, Dad, I do. You said, do you know what. I said, no Dad, what? "I keep $17 to $18 in my right front pocket. Do you know why? ' I said, no why, Dad? 'Just in case I need anything, I can walk over to the store (7-Eleven) and pick up anything I may need.' I said, oh, okay.

Then, you asked if I had your walking shoes and I said yes, Dad, I do . For some reason, I think you were worried about me since I slept in the chair next to your hospital bed. You asked if the nurses and doctors were attempting to clean my lower parts. I assured you that I was fine. I'll never forget what you said in that precious country boy stance, well, I guess we better start walking with my walking shoes. Dad, I knew instinctively in my heart that you meant that it was time to start walking on the Streets of Gold. It was time for you to go to heaven. I held back tears, because this was one walk I could not join you on at this time. However, my heart rejoiced and was and continues to be truly amazed at how God's Word (The Bible) is completely etched into your soul. The majority of the words spoken were from scripture the last few days of your life.

<u>Struggling with not being there at the Final Hour.</u>

Dad, I have played this particular scene over and over again in my head, thinking, wow, I really wanted to be there with you to hold your hand and kiss your face during your last breath. I kept beating myself up inside for not visiting you that Friday morning at 10:00 am when the Holy Spirit prompted my heart to come see you. I am learning to be a better listener now The journey was so sad, I wanted to spend some time with your grandson, running after him in the playground and listening to him speak to me in his baby language. I truly disliked the hospice nurse and did not want to see you on morphine. I realize she was doing her job, however, I do not think anyone wishes to see their love one pass away, we wanted to exhaust all resources to keep you alive and well. I personally, wanted to be able to say goodbye to my Dad without the assistance of any substances. I do realize Dad, that the substances allowed you to breathe better, as you struggled with every breath. I have forgiven myself and realized how each part of our life is orchestrated from above.

I choose to remember you the day before, beaming with your lovely smile from ear to ear when Johnny entered your hospital room. You were so glad to see him and he was honored to be there with you. Dad, this is my favorite memory of you…this is the way I choose to remember you. The precious, beautiful soul, the gentle giant who touched our lives and have made us wiser, smarter, and more determined to believe in miracles.

One of my best friend Linda called me yesterday, I forgot to let her know of your passing. When she asked how you were doing, she caught me off guard. I thought for a moment, what does she mean? Then, I explained everything that occurred fro October 2022 to March 18, 2022 at 4:30 pm. I cried profusely telling her how I felt as if I were not there for you on the final day. She said, Ann Marie, I believe your Dad did not want you to see him pass and this is why he passed away without anyone there. And, remember, everything happens for a reason, there are no mistakes. You, Ann Marie know this more than anyone. Dad, it was a though those were the words I really needed to hear. I needed to be reminded of this, my very own words that I have spoken to friends, family and love ones over the years was coming back to me by a trusted and treasured friend, who is almost like a sister to me. Marcia, who I know you know, said something quite similar and how you know how much I love you.

The 'Super' Doctor from Tufts, this is how you always referred to him…. My heart overflowed with such immense gratitude for his Eternal kindness of transferring you back to Boston in the middle of a pandemic. It is truly because of the kindness God has shown me through him that I had such a profound time being right there by your side. The "Super' Doctor told me to not 'beat myself up' and to know that you knew how much both Annette and I loved you. He said, he has never seen two (2) daughters take care of and honor their Dad the way we did.

Finally, one day, I felt as if God had given your soul 'heaven-leave' and you were standing beside me, here in my country home. I felt a sense of peace and your presence, saying, Live your life, do not feel guilty, I know how much you loved me and still do. Live your life Girl! There you go again Dad, the Papa Bear love is still reaching me from Heaven. Thank you Dad, I need to hear this to move on and live this precious gift of a life God grants each one of us.

Message of Love

My message to everyone is to love your children, young adults, who are now full grown adults, completely. Decide to listen to them, to be there for them…as you show them this example, your children will know how to truly love you.

Dad, thank you for all of the words of wisdom you shared with me and my siblings over the years. Even earlier today, as I watched this show on repairing and painting the interior part of ones home, the gentlemen explained how he painted the center window frames first as the task consumes the most time. Immediately, my mind went back to a time I was in high school… and even now, I use your advice with my own Company and working with the Consulting Firm; 'do the hardest homework first, then you may relax as you complete the easy portion. Well said and well lived, Dad! A few days ago, I wanted to pick up the phone and call you, then I looked up to heaven, with a smile on my face, knowing in my heart that you witnessed exactly what I saw, with the deer eating the cat food . How hilarious to see this large deer and her almost grown fawn, eating out of the cat's bowls. The very next day I drove into town to purchase some shelled corn for the deer and other wild life that enjoys this treat.

Another one of your sayings, is to save your pennies and if you do not touch them in a year, look at how much you'll have. I love how you and Mom never owned a credit card and only saved up your money to pay for whatever you needed in cash. How brilliant and so many Americans or people literally around the world could use such wisdom. I now save dollars this way. It does grow Dad, it certainly does. Personally, I have come to realize that every single thing we have, including our jobs, income, home, car, clothes, food, our physical body and the spirit that lives within is all from our Heavenly Father - God. Jesus explained a parable to the disciples about Minas, the importance of being responsible for the talents and gifts God gives us.

I like to use this parable and your advice to be a faithful steward with all that God has so graciously lavished upon my life. Dad, I know I have said this to you when you were here in the human form, but, I'll say it again for generations to come to read and soak into their soul of what a wondereful great, great, great, granddad they had. You, Dad are a truly wonderful human being. You were so creative and approached life as one would play a chess game. The wisdom and your ability to read people and a situation helps me navigate through the 'highways and byways' of life.I especially love how you freely told myself, Annette, Leeanne and I am sure Jianna at some point, how beautiful we are. Thank you for teaching me how to change my own spark plugs and a tire if I need to. Thank you for teaching me how to change my own oil, although, there are nice mechanics in my town that I do not mind turning over that responsibility to . They are honest and ethical people who do a great job.

<u>Laughter</u>

Dad, I have to devote the next section of this book to laughter. You were the master at making one laugh. I remember how one 'April Fools' Day, I called up on my cell phone asking you to come downstairs to open the door, as I pretended to be standing outside. You ran down the stairs, thinking I was there and realized I played the joke on you. On some level, I felt a little sad that I was not there in person to see you laugh or perhaps, the disappointment on your face when you realized I was not there to give you and Mom a hug. Or remember the time you had teased me about something and we were exchanging 'wolf tickets' meaning telling each other that we would do such and such. I'll never forget, you waited until I was fast asleep and came into my room and tied my toes together. The next morning, when I went to get out of bed, I fell to the floor. You came running down the hall laughing. I laughed as well and told you how I would tie your toes together once you were up and walking again from all that had transpired at the hospital. I wish I could tie your toes together now Dad. I remember the last week of your life, Johnny, Leeanne and Katrina came to visit with you and they had to close your hospital room door, as you had each one of them laughing so hard. See, there is that beautiful soul you have Dad, you knew that they were afraid of death and you took their mind off of the obvious by making them laugh so hard from your jokes that they were in tears.

You are my hero Dad and always shall be. God loved me so much to give me such a Dad, always thinking about how you can encourage someone. I remember one time, when we were going through a rough patch, as all children sometimes do with their parents, you asked me, 'teach me how to communicate with you.'

What a brave yet, humble question, it was so laced with love, you realizing that I was not this little girl anymore and had grown up and was a lot more educated, opinionated and sophisticated. I decided to view life with different lenses and to check my spirit to determine if I was communicating in a kinder way to you. On some level, I decided not to give my power away to people, circumstances and situations. I decided to see the goodness of God in everything. So, I invited you to come alongside me and see the wonders and goodness of God unfolding in our lives. We may both share at how during all of your life, God was right there to take very good care of you. He gave you Mom, as a wonderful, devoted wife who simply adored you and quite honestly spoiled you too much in my opinion. smile. He blessed you with four (4) healthy children, all with our own personalities and one of the most incredible Son-in-laws on this side of heaven, then with two (2) lovely grandchildren and one (1) great granddaughter, all three simply amazing human beings. We are all truly honored to be called your sons and daughters, your children, and grandchildren. We thank God for you Dad, you are truly a gem.

A Memorial in Honor of You

Well, I changed the date of your Memorial three (3) times, one or more persons had conflicts with the date. I shared with both Johnny and Annette that I planned to hold a Memorial in your honor at the Belmont Hill Club and shared how I knew that most of your friends had passed away. However, I did not care if anyone showed up besides myself, I was still going to honor your life by holding this Memorial. I went 'all out' Dad, I had such a lovely spread of food, cakes, desserts, drinks and you remember Tatyana? Yes, she flew to Boston with me, I showed her around our great city for a couple of days and then focused on planning your Memorial. Tatyana helped me set up and I am certain you were able to view from heaven how beautiful the Memorial was. I praise God for Tatyana and her friendship to you and me. She came alongside me and helped with the set-up, food, everything. I am truly blessed to have such a treasure in my life. May God bless her immensely. Just the right people showed up and it was simply beautiful. As I said during the eulogy, God gives us parents as gifts that are 'on-loan' for this lifetime, we are immensely blessed with all of their love, wisdom and kindness and then, they return to heaven. Thank you God for such great gifts!

Mischief

I loved never letting you know when I was coming to Boston and I am very thankful to Johnny for keeping it a secret all of these years. Nothing in the world may ever replace the unending expression of joy on your face and that infectious smile, beaming from ear to ear. It was the best thing ever when I showed up unannounced.

Dad, Annette shared a funny story with me of when you were teaching her how to drive. One day, she went and stole your car keys and got in your silver buick. You spotted her from the living room window and ran outside with an extra set of keys as Annette jumped out of the car, with it still running and accidentally locked the doors. You ran and opened the door, lightening fast and stopped the car before it crashed into the dumpster. Oh my goodness, the things you had to endure as a Dad. She also said that she did something wrong when she was ten (10) years old and threatened to call the police on you if you disciplined her. How funny.

Delayed

Dad, words may not express how challenging it has been for me to finish your book. My heart misses you immensely, and on some spiritual level, I do not wish to accept the fact that you are no longer with us, in the physical form. There are so many stories I wish to share. God has and continues to bless me in my career. I am working for a truly lovely Consulting firm, where the people treat each other with respect and have heart's filled with gratitude. I have time off for the Holiday's and cannot believe it is our first Holiday without you.

A cumulative snow storm has arrived, with wind chills at -40. I have been shoveling and plowing for the last three days. I know you are in heaven smiling and so proud of me. I widened my driveway by heading outside after warming up in increments. Dad, the first day the storm started, my new neighbors texted and inquired as to whether I would need help plowing the driveway, as they have a truck with a snow plow affixed to the front. I thought to myself, what kind people and then texted back to thank them and express how I have a snow plow and am all set. Three days into the storm, with blowing winds at 55 mph, and massive snow drifts, I texted them again and said, I'd take them up on their previous offer. ha ha The weather was so cold their truck was not starting.

I ended up widening the driveway on my own by plowing one spot at a time and going inside my home in-between to warm up. I know you were smiling ear to ear, as you watched from heaven. Dad, you would not believe this, however, I know you already see this from your beautiful view from above. Remember how I shared the story about the feral cats. Well, my mind was consumed on how I would help them through the winter months. I prayed and asked God for wisdom, I called my neighbor who assured me that they know instinctively how to take care of themselves in such weather. I decided to search online for feral cat houses and noticed that none were sturdy enough to ensure the cats would be warm during the winters months. I built two (2) feral cat houses for them. I added some extra hay yesterday to keep them warm. I am truly grateful for 4-H and the example of a feral cat house that was perfect for my 'fur babies'.

DadThank you for

1. Believing in me since the day I showed up on the planet.
2. For persuading me to study hard through high school and make the Honor Roll so that I'll receive a four year (4) academic scholarship.
3. For believing that I could become anything I placed my mind on becoming.
4. For believing and telling me how beautiful I am not just because I am your daughter.
5. For telling me and Annette to always be kind and respectful to guys who compliment us, even if they have not one chance in the world to date us.
6. For bringing tons of laughter into our home growing up.
7. For teaching me how to roller skate, ride my bike and scooter and how to drive. Although, the last one I know you thought at times you would head to heaven sooner. Ha ha.
8. Annette and I were reminiscing on how you would mimic the Kung Fu great master, by saying, Grasshopper, you can walk on the 'Rice Paper' of life and not fall through. Meaning, we may walk along this path called life, knowing that God is guiding and directing our every step.

9. Thank you Dad for learning the Bible inside and out. Your living example motivated me to read through the entire Bible, memorize and meditate on scriptures, which I must say is the best present a parent may impart upon their family.

10. Dad, your humility, quiet, or rather meek confidence was amazing for me to watch. You were also one of the best chefs, this side of heaven.

11. I'll never forget, one day, you came home from a long day at work, I shared about how I liked my typing class. and you surprised me with a brand new Smith Corona type writer. Remember, Dad, how you cut up a piece of cardboard, and had me copy the keys from the type writer and then practice the card board. I became one of the fastest typist in my class. Obtaining an A. The English teacher was best friends with the typing teacher, who said she believed I needed to be transferred from the General Curriculum to the College Curriculum. I transferred over and since I was so young, I did not realize, that Ms. Karen Norton, one of the Most Incredible Teachers in the World, changed my stars.

12. Dad, you were right, God prepared a way for me to succeed. Ms. Karen Norton, took me under her proverbial 'wings' and ensured I took all of the classes that would prepare me for college. You also, along with the librarian, for some reason I cannot remember her name, insisted that I attend the College Fair. During this time, I met one of the Deans from a prestigious university, who gave me his card, and said to keep up the excellent work in staying on the honor-roll and he would ensure I would receive a four (4) year academic scholarship. Tuition, books, room and board, everything, just like you spoke into my life, Dad, all this happened.

13. Thank you Dad, for planting the seed of a great life in me. Even, though, I was a teenager and at that time could not see or comprehend the 'Big picture' of Life.

14. Dad, I enjoyed all of your stories of growing up on the farm so much, that, as you know, I purchased my own little farm and have decided to include some pictures in your book, as an even further Tribute to your legacy.

15. Thank you for teaching me the 'chicken dance', it is such a great workout, now wonder you were so agile, and looked light years younger than your biological age.

16. Thank you for showing all of us what true love is by how much you missed Mom. You shared how you would dream about when you both were young and going for a walk in the park, then wake up, only to find she was not there and it was only a dream. Dad, my heart went out to you. I know God has provided a salve for your broken heart, as you are now able to see Mom in heaven, although, as you very well know, we are no longer married in heaven, however, like the angels.

17. I loved the way you spoke of your Dad, how you admired him so. I truly believe, although you lost him at the tender age of six (6), his work ethic and respect for life was certainly passed onto to you.

18. Thank you, thank you, thank you for loving me exactly as I am and for believing that I can do anything I set my mind to and that I am made perfectly.

<u>Encounter with Jesus</u>

I cherish this story my Dad shared with me when he was transferred to another hospital prior to his transfer back to Tufts Medical center. I truly believe it was a visit from Jesus Christ, our Lord, God and Savior. My Dad said a man walked past him and touched his legs and his legs immediately straightened up, enabling him to walk again. Then, the same man touched his arms and immediately he was able to lift his arms over his head and use his hands. My Dad was so excited as he expressed what occurred and I prayed with him praising God and receiving this miracle in both of our hearts and souls in the Name of Jesus. Amen! In the Bible, Jesus performed miracle upon miracle and I believe He is able to heal anyone, even now in this day and time.

<u>Words of Wisdom</u>

1. Take the trips you always wanted to take with your parents now, when they are still alive and healthy
2. Choose not to waste time disagreeing about anything. Truly, when it is all said and done the most important factor in life is Love.
3. One may never take back the words they have said to another, so be certain your words are filled with love and laced with kindness.
4. Decide to allow your parents to share their stories, their memories (without interrupting them); smile and bask in the knowing that you are giving them a chance to bask in the beauty of who all of you are collectively as a family, as a part of the bond of love.
5. Dance in the rain with your folks. Share all of the good things that are occurring in their lives and yours.
6. Tell each one how precious they are to you. Return the favor of kindness, the favor of combing his hair.
7. Sit beside his bed or chair and listen to him explain the wisdom of life. Record it, as there will be a day you wished you recorded it, just to hear your Dad's voice again.
8. Cherish, cherish, cherish them, as both your Mom and Dad did the best they could in raising you and your siblings, let them know how much you appreciate them.
9. Thank each of your parents collectively, for being there through your entire life, until they are taken up to heaven.

Civil Rights Era

Eyes who have witnessed injustice by living in the South as a young boy. Loosing your mother at birth and then your Dad to tuberculosis. Then moving to the North to escape the aftermath of slavery.

Bravery, to fall in love with and marry a full blooded Italian women. I love your heart, Dad that in-spite of all of the hatred and small minded people in the world who could not accept a race other than their own, I applaud you Dad and the countless other precious souls who decided not to look at the color of a person's skin, however, the contents of their heart. Thank you and Mom for showing us that color means nothing, we are all equal under the skies of heaven. Thank you for loving Mom, your entire life and even towards the end of your life, to see how much of a profound love Mom had on your heart and soul, brought endless tears to my eyes. I wish I could have brought her back to save you from a broken heart.

To raise mulatto kids in the days of the Civil Rights Movement, reminding each of us how God has made us perfectly. What courage and fierce bravery to show by example what is truly important in life. I am very thankful and grateful for all of the hearts out there who are like yours, you saw the beauty of ones soul, as you did with Mom and my grandmother, Anna Maria. You taught yourself Italian just to be able to speak to her, as my grandmother barely spoke English. Thank you for this beautiful tapestry of love and human kindness and respect for another. This is my prayer that the rest of the world will catch up in learning how to honor all nationalities. Every single soul has been created in the image of God and by His hands. Each soul is priceless and deserves to be honored and respected.

Tatyana, me and Johnny later in the day of after your Memorial.

One of my prayers this December 2022, was for everyone, all over the world in their families to forgive each other, to get along, be respectful and make amends, as life goes by so quickly, it is truly a gift. You and Mom showed me the importance of cherishing each moment. I had the honor to be by your bedsides when you both were leaving the planet. The two of you were and continue to be a Beautiful Gift to me and I am certain Baby Fervin, or rather, I call him my little Sweetie Pie, my little Sugar Plum, my Genius… He knows your place by the Prudential Center, whenever Fervin Sr. drives by that area, he points at your building and says, Papa….meaning you. Dad, I would have loved to see you stay longer, to spend much time and share great laughter with your grandson. He is too young, to understand, at least I think. Although, children are closer to God than we are, so, I redact my words and say, instead, that he knows very well that you are now in heaven with Jesus Christ, who is God in the Human form. I believe your grandson also knows who Mom is, as he had a chance to meet her in the spiritual form, prior to arriving here on July 23, 2019.

<u>Days Gone By</u>

Dad, I literally cannot believe you are no longer here. I miss you more than words may express. I believe there is an extra power within ones soul to allow them to be near their love ones once they have passed over into the first heaven. Sometimes, as I sit here, I feel your presence, your smile, your laughter, a funny thought a treasured memory. I praise God for allowing you to visit with us. Annette has shared similar stories as well as Leeanne feeling the same presence. I know it is you, Dad, expressing your love and care for us even from so far. How is it to be beside the love of your life? Give her a big hug and kiss from us and let her know that we love her immensely as well. Often, I wake up, especially on the weekends and thank God for the morning and ask him to send you and Mom a kiss and hug from me.

I did not even plant a garden this Spring, as it was too much for me to bear without having you here to share the stories with. Life is truly a treasure, a gift…we do not stop to realize it enough. Sometimes, we are so caught up in the moment of whatever may be occurring without cherishing a smile, or listening to you sing or do your 'chicken dance'. Dad, I struggle with the way you exited this world. I often have conversations with God about it. I wish you did not have the accident and that you were able to walk, talk and do the things you loved. I wish you were healthy and strong as you were in days gone by. I wish Mom were alive and well and completely healthy so that the two of you could grow into your Golden year's together.

Endless Tears

Dad, some days, I cannot stop crying. I held off writing your book because I simply did not wish to cry anymore. I have decided to make a vow to God to write three (3) hours each Saturday, or Shabbat as you remember to complete your book. A few minutes ago, I started crying and then the phone rang and yes, you have guessed it, your little grandson on Facetime showing me the house and bridge he is building. What a priceless little one, he is. You were absolutely correct when you told Annette how he is going to be so much fun.

We will all remember how you told him on Facetime from your hospital bed, as he was crying, 'I am going to put you in my pocket'. He stopped crying to listen to his Papa. Here is sending you a kiss from him and all of us, FOREVER! We miss you Dad and love you immensely.

Thank you, a word you said often in the last days of your life. As though you wanted those words to stay etched in my soul, in Johnny's soul, Annette's soul, Fervin Sr's soul. As I gave you a cough drop, held the glass of apple juice so you may sip through the straw, fed you your meal, all that came from your heart and out of your mouth was a faint, yet, most precious, Thank You.

Dad, it was my true honor to do these simple, yet truly significant acts of love and kindness for you. All my life you have believed in me, whatever idea, thought or adventure I had in my heart, you were there, smiling, telling me to go on, soar like the eagles.

Your little three (3) year old grandson just called me a few minutes ago to show me his finger. He has a little paper cut from the ironing board. I asked him to hold his finger to the phone and I kissed it to make it better.

Dad, you may have no idea of how much I wanted God to make everything better. How I prayed everyday, several times throughout the day along with fasting every Wednesday and Thursday along with some precious friends of mine who were so honorable to pray and fast with me.

Dad, as you have said to me often, and I have come to realize this for myself, life is a beautiful journey. Almost as if, life were a tapestry of which God grants us beautiful souls, of which I am eternally grateful for you and Mom. These beautiful souls walk along side your life for a set period of time, pouring there precious words of wisdom, discernment, insight and understanding into your heart and soul.. Each precious word drenched in love. Thank you, Dad for sharing such wisdom.

Dad, there is a Christian radio station, I listen to often, and one of the story tellers share the significance of the word, 'Thank You', how it means that someone wants to stop, and take notice, to express their gratitude of one doing something kind for the other. Each time, I listen, it never fails, my eyes fill with tears and my heart and soul goes back to those presumably endless days sitting by your hospital bed, hearing you say Thank you.

Dad, I remember my first indoctrination to credit cards, even though you and Mom never owned a credit card or checking account. As a young girl, I never really liked Christmas, as our neighbors, who had five (5) or six (6) kids would always seem to have lots of toys and new clothes.

You must have overheard me talking to Mom one day and then chimed in stating how just because those people seem as though they are wealthy, you knew for a fact that they had maxed out their credit cards, of which they had several and were barely living from pay check to pay check. I had no idea. What a powerful financial lesson, which changed my perspective for the rest of my life. I, only pay for things I have budgeted for. My one credit card is paid off monthly, enabling me to never have to incur finance charges. I admire how wise you were Dad. I believe, on some level, growing up on the farm in Kelford, North Carolina has taught you these valuable life lessons. This is most likely how your Dad was able, and I am certain his Dad, and his Dad's Dad, were able to own all that land and have six (6) or more houses deeded to you, once you became an adult.

Since, we grew up in such humble beginnings, I make this declaration each day on how Generational blessings are in our family to stay and I offer up prayers of gratitude to God for such blessings. God owns it all anyhow. Granting man with wisdom to build houses, banks, skyscrapers, airplanes, etc. God endows each of us with great wisdom, knowledge and intelligence, as we take time to go within.

I AM THE DAUGHTER OF A KING WHO IS NOT MOVED BY THE WORLD

FOR MY GOD IS WITH ME AND GOES BEFORE ME I DO NOT FEAR FOR I AM HIS

I remember and cherish this one saying you said to me as a young girl and would smile such a lovely smile when I quoted it back to you over the years. "Whatever you are fearful of, master it so that it does not master you." Wow! Dad, such powerful words of wisdom! I quote this often when I might be a little uncertain. I pray, laying my request before the throne of God and watch in eager expectation as He directs my steps and allows my dreams to unfold in His appointed time.

Thank you, Dad for your example during my teenage years as well of how you memorized scripture in the bible and made it a part of your soul. I had to include this picture, as I believe it is just as powerful as the quote of mastering anything I may be fearful of. These days, Praise God, I lift my eyes to Him. He takes care of everything. I love you, Dad, FOREVER! Thank you for loving all of us enough to share life truths, God's truth with us, so we may navigate ourselves through life in a way, engulfed by God's Favor, Love, Abundance, Protection, Great Health and Kindness.

<u>Not ready to say goodbye.</u>

Your Best Friend

Dad, you were my best friend as a child growing up. We took endless fishing trips together. Dad, who will place the bait on my fishing hook now? I, want to say thank you again for always bating my fishing hook for me. Never, once did you say, even as I went fishing with you as an adult, Ann Marie, bait your own hook. No instead, you would bait mine, then yours, I would cast out my line and then you would cast out your line, and we would take in the beautiful scenery. Those were the simple days, the days filled with sunshine and happiness. I loved going Deep Sea Fishing as well. Now, as tribute to you, I plan to take a Whale Watching trip in the Spring to Salute You, Dad, for introducing me to fishing and teaching me to appreciate the ebb and flow of life by watching the tide. 'Take life in stride, Ann Marie.'

Teaching me when the fish would bite, on cooler days they would come up to the surface. I cherish the smell of the sea, the seagulls, although most Bostonians attempt to chase them away. Their call reminds me of days gone by, days fishing with you. Sunrises and sunsets are some of the best in the world by the ocean. I must say, I did not always like having to get up at 2;30 am to meet the ferry at 3:30 am in Woodshole to catch the Deep Sea fishing ship, however, I knew you would not mind if I fell asleep until we arrived. Dad, I am Not ready to say Goodbye.

Remember when we were all fishing off of the side of the ship, I thought I was reeling in a fish, however, it was so strong that it took three (3) fishermen and yourself to hold onto me so that I would not go overboard. You reeled in the fish, which happened to be a baby shark. This was the talk of the ship, everyone was amazed that I had held on for so long.

I personally, was grateful for all the kind fishermen. To this day, if I am traveling throughout the U.S. or in another country or continent, when I see a fisherman, I'll go over and ask what kind of fish are in those waters and whether he or she has caught anything. One year, when I was in Paris for work, over the weekend, one of my colleagues and I were walking along the seashore, as it was close to Christmas, there was a fisherman.

Dad, you could tell by the lines on his face that he was a sea frarer most of his life. I shared with my colleague how I went fishing with you most of my life and would be a minute as I wanted to speak with the fisherman. He was truly kind and said that pullock were bountiful there. Dad, I find fisherman to be down to earth and most truly appreciative of the beauty of nature. On some level, as I travel, these fisherman keep the memory of you alive.

I wish all children may have a precious memory of going fishing with their Dad.

You were a truly good Dad, always teaching us about life. The way you interacted with the other fishermen, in kindness, at the seashore, there were no disputes on race, color, profession or status. Each precious soul came to fish and soak in the beauty of the horizon, marvel at the height of the waves and how blue the ocean was as it reflected the radiant colors of the sky.

Never, once in all the years we went fishing did one fisherman ever ask where we were from, what we did for a living. In todays world, there are some who are consumed with the shallow things of life. Hopefully, for their sake, one day they will stumble across true beauty, true meaning as we have.

Here is a really lovely picture of Annette and Fervin, your sweet youngest daughter and an incredible son-in-law, both who love you forever!!!!

Dad, I had to include this incredible picture of the sunrise in dedication
to your memory and legacy. I know how you loved sunrises.
An awesome picture of the sunrise one wintery morning on the farm.

Dad, this is a picture of the moon rising from the East one evening. Isn't it beautiful? I included it as you would always say, how we are looking up at the same moon.

Here is a picture of your little grandson, he is three (3) years old now. This is him on vacation in the D.R. for the Christmas holidays. I pray that his Dad takes him fishing when he is a little older.

He is asking his Mommy and Daddy to read to him. I plan t purchase a little firetruck book and read with him when he calls me on FaceTime. On Saturday, I noticed I missed a FaceTime call from him. I called back and he explained how his Papa (meaning grad dad, Fervin, Sr's Dad, and Grandma gave him a croissant. In his attempt to share a bite with me via FaceTime, he dropped it on the porch. Annette, picked it up and told him he could not eat it, since it was now 'dirty'. The little guy went downstairs to his grandma and knocked on the door, when she opened it, he explained to her in Spanish how he needed another as his first one fell. Dad, his is almost four (4) years old now and I am in Awe of this little genius,speaking two languages, fluently.

I believe God gave us little Fervin, as a gift, to lessen the pain in our hearts from loosing you and Mom too soon.

The Best Dad that Ever Lived. Thank you, Thank you, Thank you for sharing your life with me. Thank you for teaching me so many wise words of wisdom. Thank you for teaching me how to travel through life by teaching myself how to move forward, learn new things and to be happy.

Psalm 145

Dad, to say you are truly missed does not even begin to equate to how I, Annette, Johnny, Fervin Sr, little Fervin, Leeanne, Katrina, Elizabeth, Jianna, Marcia, Rikki and Tatyana feel of not having you here.

I am not sure if you are able to read these pages from Heaven, or how everything works up there, however, to me, you were the perfect Dad who did not allow the circumstances of your life to snuff out your light. God allowed you and Mom to meet, only to spend 60 years together. What an incredible God, knowing that you needed to feel loved and part of a family,

Thank you, Dad for always being there to listen to all of us. I was and still am truly amazed at your patience and willingness to listen.

In my opinion, you are truly a Genius. You taught yourself how to rebuild car engines, taught yourself to read better by purchasing used encyclopedia's at a second hand store. You, Dad were a self- made person, indeed. I love you Forever!!!!!

Dad, I just love this picture and had to include it in this book to allow your grand children and great grand children to see your incredible smile at the age of seven-teen (17).

I have a saying, that country boys (men) are incredibly smart. I truly believe you were a genius. Men growing up in the country have to figure out how to fix the plow and all sorts of things on the farm, most often with no help, often times in frigid weather.

I, personally love living out in the country. I love growing my vegetables from seed. The taste is so different from store bought regular and some organic vegetables, nothing truly can compare. This explains why you were so strong. As strong as an Ox, as you would say. You grew up on fresh vegetables, animals from the farm, fruit trees such as apples, and peaches. You had walnut and pecan trees on your land as well. I plan to plant a pecan tree this summer in honor of you, since you always asked when are you going to plant a pecan tree.

Thank you for taking me on my first plane ride to Kelford, North Carolina at the age of 11 to meet my aunt, Ms. Katie Bishop and her family. What extraordinary individuals, I wish I had spent more time with them. It would be nice to be able to press a "rewind' button to spend more time with those we love.

ACKNOWLEDGEMENTS

I would like to thank God for all of the times you, Dad said, 'Ann Marie, you need to write a book, why not publish the books you have already written'. I believe on some level, you and Mom are able to see me from heaven and rejoiced with me two (2) days ago, as I self-published my first two (2) books I have written, (I Love You Mom - Forever and 365 Days of Infinite Wishes and Wisdom). Thank you for always believing in me. I wish circumstances were different for this book. I wish you were here.

Thank you to Bonnie Olson Kramer for insisting on my publishing the book to share with the world. Bonnie, the gift of your friendship, support and words of wisdom are truly remarkable.

Thank you Dad (who's in Heaven) for placing all of this love in my heart and soul to radiate out into the world. Thank you Dad for loving Mom regardless of your ethnicity and showing me to do the same, to love and respect people of all nationalities. You truly are the most Incredible Dad Ever!!!!!

My Wish

It is my hearts desire and fervent wish that whoever reads this book will feel the immense love my Dad poured into my and my siblings souls during his lifetime. I pray that each one of you would experience, give and receive the undying love that is a gift from above. May you experience this love in all of your relationships, to believe in, speak words of encouragement and strength into your children's lives, into your parent's lives, into your spouses life, into your friends and neighbors lives; and yes, into your own life. God Bless You!

ABOUT THE AUTHOR

She wishes to take a moment to honor the life of her precious Dad. Recalling the importance of expressing to ones parents how much you love and appreciate all that they have done for you. To treat them with great respect, especially in their senior years, when they need you the most,

Printed in the United States
by Baker & Taylor Publisher Services